A Pocket Guide

to

Small Business Success

Rob England

Copyright © 2015 by Robert England
All rights reserved.
ISBN: 1511884908
ISBN-13: 978-1511884907

Contents

	Introduction	3
1.	Before you start	6
2.	Money	24
3.	People	44
4.	Sales and Marketing	56
5.	Running it	72
6.	Ongoing Strategy	90
7.	Selling it	98
8.	Remember…	106

Introduction

I'm not one of these TV multi-millionaire dragons, more interested in their TV and public profiles than their next pay cheque. I'm not glamorous, I'm not fit, I'm not on the telly, but I have been running small businesses for the last twenty years and I have sold the last two successfully for a profit.

Most people running small businesses are the same; they're normal people, with normal lives, normal kids and they're not multi-millionaires either, so I can completely relate to them.

I was lucky enough to make enough money when I sold my last business to be semi-retired before the age of 50 and now I spend my time helping other small businesses to grow and succeed. When you've been through the journey, from start-up to shit street, brought in new investment in order to survive, diversified when the Government changed all the rules and threatened to squash you, come through the other side and then finally sold it, it's amazing what you learn and what you know. In fact, you don't realise just how much you do know, but I've been amazed at how little some owners of businesses still on the journey know, how unaware they are of their own business and therefore their own life, and how naïve they can be commercially.

That said, I know only too well how easy it is to be so engrossed in your own business that you can't see the wood for the trees, where the obvious solutions are completely hidden away somewhere in the forest. I also know, from experience, how helpful it is to have an outsider to bounce ideas off, get a new perspective from and help clear the trees out of the way to allow you to see the way forward.

So, during the retired half of semi-retired, I decided to write this book; for the thousands of normal people who run their own businesses, from a normal person. Real world examples are included throughout and there is a recap of the salient points at the end of each chapter.

It passes on some of the things I've learned over the years and will prevent you from making some of the mistakes I've made along the way, so long as you at least take some notice!

Good luck with your endeavours.

/1
Before you start

Why?

If you're thinking of starting your own business, first of all ask yourself why you're doing it. There are many reasons why people start a business; it may be:

- to build something, sell it and make your millions
- to escape a horrible boss in your current dead-end job
- because you think you can do it better than anyone else
- because you've thought of a great idea and no-one else is doing it
- to have freedom, make your own decisions and not be answerable to anyone else
- to have freedom and pick and choose when you work
- to pay yourself whatever you choose
- or a host of other reasons

It may be one of these reasons or a combination of them, but what I can tell you straight away is that if you're thinking of starting a small business, don't do it for the salary.

Running your own business is not easy; it demands long hours, lots of commitment, creates risk, worry, stress and imposes lots of responsibility. Start a business to create something, to build something of long term value and to have freedom and choice and you'll be on the right lines.

If you're starting a business for the salary, just go and get a job and work for someone else instead. It's far simpler, less risky, more secure and has less responsibility. If it's all about the salary, don't put yourself through the aggravation that goes with a business.

They say people who start their own business just want to work 100 hours a week so nobody else can tell them what to do, so it has to be about much more than the salary.

When you work for someone else and you never have to make the decisions or carry the can, it's always easier to make the best choices because you don't have to live with them and you can live in an ideal world. Business isn't an ideal world and you will rarely encounter the ideal circumstances when there is enough cash to pay for the right choices, or the right staff to carry out the right initiatives. It's a world full of compromises and tough choices, so be prepared for it.

If you're doing it to pick and choose when you work, then you're most likely to work longer hours than you've ever worked before and half your weekends too. If you're doing it to pay yourself whatever you'd like, then I hope you're successful enough to be able to do it, because in most small businesses the boss comes last on the list of people to be paid; after the staff, the creditors, the taxman and everyone else. Hopefully, there will always be enough cash available to pay everyone else and pay yourself what you'd like, but when times are tough, be prepared to suffer financially.

If you're doing it so you're not answerable to anyone else, that's fine, but be prepared for a lonely life sometimes, because there'll be nobody to talk to, discuss problems with or share the load with; it's all down to you.

So, think about why you're doing it, where you'd like to end up, and then work on how you'll get there.

It's really about the three R's

In the old days at school the three R's were reading, writing and arithmetic, but if you decide to start a new business, then the three R's are what it's really all about; Risk, Responsibility and Reward.

You have to take the risk of investing or raising the money in order to start the business, maybe giving up a secure job and having a go at something that statistically has a good chance of failing, possibly even risking the family home and bankruptcy. You have to accept the responsibility for everything that goes on in the business, most importantly all the difficult things, all the decisions and you have to accept that ultimately everything comes back to you.

Accepting the responsibility is probably the biggest R you have to take. You are responsible for making sure the staff get paid every week or every month, making sure enough sales come in, making sure the costs are controlled, making sure people get what they need in order to do their job, making sure the customers are happy and that everything stays within the law. You're the one who has to make and carry out the difficult things, go and beg the bank for more money or more time, be the nasty horrible boss that sacks somebody who isn't good enough and put them out of a job or not give someone a pay rise when they expect it but don't deserve it.

If you're happy to take the risks and are prepared to accept the responsibility, then it's only right that you should enjoy the rewards. No one will put more on the line than you do, so no one should ultimately benefit more than you do.

Unfortunately, the rewards come last and they may be a long way away in the future, so you have to be prepared to go through the pain before you get to enjoy the rewards of your endeavours. The chances are it won't be an easy ride and it may well be rocky and a bit of an adventure, but as all entrepreneurs starting out hope, it will be worth it in the end.

Research and the Business Plan

If you've had the big idea and you've decided to start your own business, you need to do as much research as possible into what you're going to do and then project what you think it will cost and how much profit it can make.

Look at how big the market is, who the competitors are, what similar products sell for and think about how you might be different and better. Ultimately, you need to create a business plan with as much thought and as much detail as you can, and then a spreadsheet to plug all the numbers into to see if it's likely to be profitable.

> A guy is looking to start his own business selling 3-D printing designs over the internet. He's hoping that the growth of 3-D printing over the next five years will be exponential and he has a point: 3-D printing will change our lives, particularly in manufacturing.
>
> For example, say you need a plastic spatula to cook dinner; rather than buying one from a shop, you'll be able to download a template and print your own.

> Already, in China, they are 3-D printing 10 porta-cabin style houses a day - imagine the impact of that on the construction industry.
>
> Considering the increase in users of 3-D printers, the guy has to work out who is likely to have access to a 3-D printer and who is going to buy his designs. Given that he's an engineer and is interested in furthering the knowledge and educating people in the mechanics and reasoning behind engineering, students of the subject are a prime target for him. So, what are the questions to ask?
>
> - How many universities are there in the UK that offer engineering degrees?
> - How many different courses are there?
> - How many people are taken on to each course?
> - Multiply that by 3 as it's a 3 year course, so there are always three groups taking it at the different stages.
>
> That should provide the target population of (only) students that ought to be interested in his products. However, it's an internet business so it's not restricted to the UK, so also go around Europe and the USA, work out those numbers too, add them all together and get excited.

It's always easy to get excited about the sales numbers, but they are the ones that are hardest to predict and the ones that are so variable.

You also have to research the other side of the business, the costs. These are far more predictable and tend to be fixed and regular, needing to be paid every month, regardless of sales.

Break the costs down in to headings such as:
- Salaries (don't forget to add 13.8% for employers National Insurance contributions, which can add almost £10,000 per annum to a salary bill of just £5k per month)
- Rent and Rates (business rates can sometimes be about the same as the rent, so double the rent)
- Gas, Water and Electricity
- Telephone bill (businesses can eat the telephone!)
- Travel and Expenses
- Insurances
- Marketing (now there's a black hole for a salesman)
- Professional fees (your accountant will want to be paid for doing your year-end figures)
- Finance charges, including bank charges, credit card charges, Paypal costs, etc. A credit card handling fee of 2% comes straight off the margin generated from the sale and if your gross margin is 25% equates to losing 8% of your profit.
- Website costs, including building it in the first place, can run into thousands. Don't build your own unless you really are a website designer, you can always tell and it looks amateur.

- Plant, machinery and any equipment you need to purchase to be able to create your products.
- Consultancy fees, for people like me to help you get it right.

	Month 1	Month 2	➡	Month 12	Total
SALES					
Category 1	-	-	...	-	-
Category 2	-	-	...	-	-
Category 3	-	-	...	-	-
TOTAL SALES	-	-	...	-	-
COST OF SALES					
Category 1	-	-	...	-	-
Category 2	-	-	...	-	-
Category 3	-	-	...	-	-
TOTAL COST OF SALES	-	-	...	-	-
GROSS PROFIT	-	-	...	-	-
EXPENDITURE					
Salaries	-	-	...	-	-
Commission	-	-	...	-	-
Travel & Expenses	-	-	...	-	-
Pensions	-	-	...	-	-
Plant & Machinery	-	-	...	-	-
Delivery	-	-	...	-	-
Web Hosting	-	-	...	-	-
Office Consumables	-	-	...	-	-
Bank Charges	-	-	...	-	-
Rent and Rates	-	-	...	-	-
Subscriptions	-	-	...	-	-
Insurances	-	-	...	-	-
Marketing	-	-	...	-	-
Printing	-	-	...	-	-
Professional Fees	-	-	...	-	-
Consultancy	-	-	...	-	-
Telephones	-	-	...	-	-
Miscellaneous	-	-	...	-	-
TOTALS	-	-	...	-	-
NET PROFIT	-	-	...	-	-
RUNNING TOTAL	-	-	...	-	-

Sample layout for a Profit and Loss projection

It's really important to get the costs right and as accurate as possible. It can also be quite scary once they've been added up for the year, and it's not difficult for a company of just four or five people to cost in excess of £200,000 a year. Almost £20,000 every month, out of your own pocket, with no questions asked, no excuses and without fail. Are you ready for this?

The biggest single cost is usually people, so be really careful and question yourself when thinking about who you need to begin with. I've often seen people leave big corporate companies, with thousands of people and someone for everything, and start businesses with way too many staff that they simply can't afford. It's easy to say you need an administrator or a receptionist because everyone has those, but you've just added £30,000 to the annual salary bill. Have them by all means, but only if you're prepared to pay that money out of your own pocket, before you pay yourself, because that's where the money is now coming from. If your product makes you £100 every time you sell it, you need to sell 300 more every year just to pay for those people, and it'll be hard enough to sell any at all in the first few months.

Look at how the business can be funded; if you have a lump sum to invest, try and make it last as long as possible because you'll need the cash to keep you going until the sales start to roll in. If you need to buy equipment worth £10,000 to get going, try and borrow the money or lease the equipment, so you don't use £10,000 of your capital up in the first month.

Think carefully about marketing and how to get the most out of it for the least cost. It's great to have full colour glossy adverts in magazines, but they are notoriously expensive and most people just look at the picture and turn the page. Nowadays Facebook, Twitter and the social networks offer a cheap or even free route to market that can hit an awful lot of people very quickly. It doesn't have to cost lots of money. Remember, though, that nobody knows you're there when you open for business unless you tell them you are.

Once you've got the costs worked out, you can go back to the sales side of the equation and work out how much you need to sell to be profitable.

But be careful, because…

Projections are always wrong

One thing that is pretty much guaranteed is when you come up with your initial projections, however careful you are and however much care you've taken to get them right, they'll be wrong.

Usually, it's the sales side of things that people get completely wrong, because in simple terms things just take time. The enthusiasm and optimism that goes with starting a new business makes people think "I'll be able to get that deal", or "I can sell six of those a month, no problem", and usually, that's just what it is, enthusiasm and optimism. There's nothing wrong with it, everybody has it, but the reality is that things just take longer than we hope or would like.

> Charities are usually governed by a Board of Trustees who meet quarterly. A company which sells to a charity puts a proposal forward to the next Trustees meeting for approval. Their projections have the deal

> in the current month. The meeting over-runs and the proposal is carried over to the next meeting as an outstanding item. As a result, the supplier has to wait for the order; not their fault, nothing they can do, but their projections have completely gone to pot, and the £35k order they were expecting imminently has to wait for another three months.

It's simple human nature and normal life that mess up your projections; people are off sick, go on holiday, are too busy doing more important things to bother signing your order, and whilst it will be your top priority, it won't be theirs because it means they're having to spend money and we tend to avoid that for as long as possible if we can.

A simple rule of thumb is to come up with your initial projections, having thought them through and been as conservative as possible, then **halve your sales** (yes, halve your sales), **add 20% to your costs** and you might be close to getting it right. Don't forget to consider VAT, because if you don't intend to register for it, you won't be able to claim back the VAT on things you buy. Unlike the consumer world, the business world often quotes prices exclusive of VAT, but if you're not registered, you'll have to pay it and everything will cost you 20% more than you may have initially thought.

At this point, you might have a good idea how much capital you will need to start with. You may also realise that you don't have enough money yourself and need to go out and raise some more. That, in itself, is difficult because the banks no longer take risks, so it's vital to try and make your own money last as long as possible in this pre-start stage. You'll go back and look at the costs again, question whether you can do without an extra member of staff for a couple of months to save money, and be more prudent than before, but it's good to keep re-visiting the projections until you can live with them. You are, after all, going to have to live with them every day.

If you haven't got enough money

Once you have the initial spreadsheet completed, it should tell you how much you will need to launch the business, or at least how much you will need until sales pick up sufficiently that you don't have to fund things any more. If you've used something like the spreadsheet I've shown earlier in the section, then the Running Total at the very bottom will normally show a minus figure (of initial setup costs and early losses) and then come back up to positive as increased sales kick in after the initial expense of setting up the business.

If you're happy and comfortable with your projections, you should now know where you stand; you know how much money the business needs initially and you know how much of your own money you have to put into it. If you've got enough, then great, but it's often the case that additional funds are needed to get a business off the ground. There are lots of different ways to raise this initial money and largely it depends on how comfortable you are with the options you could consider. People borrow it from friends and family, re-mortgage their house, go to the bank, crowd-funding is becoming more popular nowadays, there are grants and loans available from various government agencies and councils, and there are also outside investors.

The next chapter deals with Money and discusses the options for raising it.

What's it look like when it's finished?

This should be a continual process really, but I always ask people "what's it look like when it's finished?" How do you see your business at the point where you'll be happy to say *"I did it!"*?

- How big will it be?
- What kind of premises will you be in?
- How profitable will it be?
- What kind of position will it hold in its marketplace?
- What role will you still play?
- Who'll still be with you?
- How rich will you be?

It's good to have that kind of vision or dream of what your business will look like at the point you're happy; after all, if you don't know where you're going you're unlikely to get there and it will be much harder to take anybody with you. It also allows you to create measurable steps along the way and help you keep progress in your thoughts. You can make sure you're getting there, if only in your head and adjust your plans accordingly.

It doesn't really matter how large or small the vision is – as long as there is one.

> I saw my own business in a modern two storey office building with around thirty staff, a team of ten software developers, four to six helpdesk staff, half a dozen trainers out on the road seeing customers, training facilities so we could hold our own courses, a

> good marketing team and ethical sales people who wouldn't sell things we couldn't deliver. Just as importantly, I wanted us to have an excellent reputation so we could hold our heads up high, derived from having a great product, providing great service and being recognised by everyone around us as being the best in our markets.
>
> In my head, I had us turning over two and a half to three million pounds a year, around 60% of which came from recurring revenues and making net profits of between 15% and 20% of turnover.

As you can see, I had the vision and I knew where I was going. My decisions were always geared to the impact they would have in achieving those long term goals, rather than the immediate or short term.

Some people will gear their vision to more material things, rather than to the business itself; they'll think about the big house they'd like, the fancy car they'll drive, the holiday home they might buy and so on. That's fine on an individual basis and we all have our hopes and dreams, but there needs to be a vision for the business too, because it's the business that will allow the personal dreams to be realised. If the business has no direction, no targets to aim at, then it's unlikely the personal dreams will be realised.

The chances are you'll never achieve your ultimate ambitions. You may well achieve your original ones, but by the time you get to them, you'll have moved them and reset them to a higher point, and when you get to those you'll have moved them on again to a higher point still. People often say we never achieve our ambitions, because we always keep pushing them further out in front of us.

Ironically, I got about half way to mine when the phone rang one day and the caller said "Hi Rob, I'd like to buy your business". At the time we had no thought or intention of selling and the rest, as they say, is history. I never got to fully realise my vision for the company, but it was important to have that vision and those targets to aim for.

Before you start Recap

- Ask yourself why you're doing it
- Remember the three R's – risk, responsibility and reward
- Do your research, thoroughly
- Create projections you can live with
- Find out how much money you'll need
- What's it look like when it's finished?
- Set your targets

/2
Money

Your research and the Business Plan should tell you how much money the business will need in the first few months until sales come in and turn it to profitability. Very few businesses are lucky enough to be profitable really quickly and the setup and running costs will need to be covered before the sales pipeline starts to pay all the bills.

The projections will have shown how much money is needed and if you can cover that yourself, then great. If it needs more, then you will need to raise it from other sources. There are various ways of raising the extra money and some of them are discussed in this chapter.

How to structure your capital

If it's a limited company you're creating, the owners technically have to buy the shares in the company. Many companies have a nominal £2 or £100 of share capital, and that's fine in a privately owned small company. You may have 2 or 100 £1 shares and you spend your private money buying those shares from the company.

Any new business will undoubtedly need more funding than that, so let's say the business needs £20,000 in order to get it going and you have that to inject yourself. You could increase the share capital and have 20,000 £1 shares, but once you've bought those shares, you can't easily get the money back out of the business in a tax efficient way. You could pay yourself more, or give yourself more dividends based on profit, but you'll pay tax and/or National Insurance contributions on those amounts.

It's much better to structure your capital as a nominal number of shares and the rest as a loan from you to the business. You could do it, for example, as £1,000 of share capital (1,000 shares at £1 each) and then £19,000 of loan without any fixed term on it. In this way, as soon as the company can afford it, it can make loan repayments to you and you can have the £19,000 back tax-free, recovering most of your initial outlay in a tax efficient way. If you need external investment, then any investor, particular a private one, would in all likelihood want to structure their investment in the same way. If you can get your money back out tax-free, then why shouldn't they?

The downside to this arrangement is that the company's accounts will carry a long term debt (to you) and look like the business owes money, which technically it does. This may have an impact if your suppliers want to look at your accounts before giving you credit, for example, but remember that ultimately as the owner and shareholder, you're the only one that has to be comfortable with it and you're doing it this way for your own benefit. If you've set yourself up for PAYE as well, you could even take the loan repayments in lieu of salary, further saving the income tax and NI contributions on your salary.

In the initial stages of the business you'll need all the cash you've got and giving it away to the taxman serves no purpose at all, so avoid it if you can, but without breaking the law and landing yourself in trouble.

Know your numbers

We've all seen budding entrepreneurs being quizzed on Dragons Den about their businesses and I'm always staggered by how many simply don't know their numbers. What did you turnover last year? How much profit did you make? What's your gross margin? All very standard questions, but people continue to embarrass themselves.

I watched a TV programme recently where the Sales and Marketing Director took two samples of his product to a prospective client and didn't even know the selling price of the second product! Let me just run that by you again; he was the Sales and Marketing Director and he didn't even know how much his own product sold for! He even had the nerve to complain that he hadn't had much time to prepare! Shoot him; if not that, please at least sack him. He looked like such an amateur you wouldn't buy from him in a month of Sundays.

If a bank or an investor is going to back an entrepreneur, the one thing they need to have is confidence. If you can't even tell them how much you turned over, how much profit you made, how much your costs are or what margins you make, don't expect them to take you seriously. If you don't even know what you do with your own money, do you think a bank or investor will think you'll know what you're doing with theirs?

The owner of a small business should know their business inside out, so if you can't even tell someone the basic details, you have no credibility. When I'm advising a business, some of the very first questions I ask are about their numbers. The questions aren't necessarily simply about the turnover, they tend to be more about what specific items they sell, in what quantities, and how much margin each one makes.

If you don't know your numbers, you might be spending more money in salaries and marketing trying to sell a product that actually makes you nothing. You will certainly not be maximising the potential of the business and you'll undoubtedly be making life more difficult for yourself.

As a minimum, you should know the following:
- Annual turnover
- Cost of sales
- Gross margin
- Salaries
- Other costs
- Net profit
- %age of turnover for each product
- How many of each product you sell

Where to find your numbers:

	Month 1	➡	Month 12	Total	
SALES					
Category 1	-	...	-	-	
Category 2	-	...	-	-	
Category 3	-	...	-	-	
TOTAL SALES	-	...	-	-	**Turnover**
COST OF SALES					
Category 1	-	...	-	-	
Category 2	-	...	-	-	
Category 3	-	...	-	-	
TOTAL COST OF SALES	-	...	-	-	**Cost of Sales**
GROSS PROFIT	-	...	-	-	**Gross Margin**
EXPENDITURE					
Salaries	-	...	-	-	**Salaries**
Commission	-	...	-	-	
Travel & Expenses	-	...	-	-	
Pensions	-	...	-	-	
Plant & Machinery	-	...	-	-	
Delivery	-	...	-	-	
Web Hosting	-	...	-	-	
Office Consumables	-	...	-	-	
Bank Charges	-	...	-	-	**Other Costs**
Rent and Rates	-	...	-	-	
Subscriptions	-	...	-	-	
Insurances	-	...	-	-	
Marketing	-	...	-	-	
Printing	-	...	-	-	
Professional Fees	-	...	-	-	
Consultancy	-	...	-	-	
Telephones	-	...	-	-	
Miscellaneous	-	...	-	-	
TOTALS	-	...	-		
NET PROFIT	-	...	-	-	**Profit**
RUNNING TOTAL	-	...	-	-	

I tend to take the numbers game down to a further level of detail and look at the effectiveness of products and even sales people, and I cover that in the chapter on Sales and Marketing.

If you don't know the numbers;
- how can you identify the problems?
- how can you make sure you have the right cost base?
- how can you know what really makes you money?
- you don't know what's going on in your own business and you can't manage it effectively.

Not knowing your own numbers is just embarrassing, plain and simple.

Banks don't take risks

It's a real shame we need to have bank accounts, because most of the high street banks are useless. The irony is that they are supposed to look after our money, but they charge us a fortune for doing it and sometimes won't even let us get at it when we want it.

After the financial crash in the late noughties, modern day banks no longer take risks. Not surprisingly, they are out to look after themselves, and whilst they will talk a good talk in terms of helping and lending small businesses money, you may find that things are different once you actually go and ask for it. They will certainly want a detailed Business Plan before considering lending, so you need to make sure you have a coherent plan in place to take with you. This just covers the back of the Manager you see and shows that they have listened, got the details and have filed the paperwork.

It's very unlikely a bank would inject capital into a business; they would usually offer either a loan, to be repaid over a period of time, or a simple overdraft, so you can dip into it as and when you need it. Generally speaking, if the money is only required for the short term, then an overdraft is the way to go as it's more temporary and you'll only pay interest on it when you use it, rather than all the time with a loan.

Ultimately, the lending decision will probably be the responsibility of a computer, which hasn't read the plan, doesn't know who you are, doesn't like you and doesn't care whether it lends you the money or not. Gone are the days of looking the Bank Manager in the eye, promising to be a responsible adult with his money and paying him back.

If you get to the position where you need fairly substantial funds, the bank will require security from you so their debt is safe. This will take the form of you signing legal papers which allow the bank to take hold of your possessions should you default on the loan or overdraft and cannot afford to pay them back in the normal way. Typically, however, our largest asset tends to be our home and so the bank will look to take a charge over your home, giving them the right to take it from you and sell it in order to recover their debt should you default.

This is the one aspect of borrowing money for a business that tends to worry people the most, especially spouses! If the business fails, then the house could be gone and you could theoretically be homeless. The reality is slightly different and the bank will actually do whatever they can to recover their money in other ways, so they don't have to take your house. They do at least have some compassion. For example, a re-mortgage on the house would be looked at first so that you end up with a larger monthly mortgage payment instead. I've even known people lodge savings accounts with the bank, so they can recover the money that way, although this isn't a great idea as they'll wonder why you want to borrow their money when you've got the savings tucked away and could have used your own instead.

Yes, it's a worry providing security to the bank via your home. I would certainly avoid it wherever possible for obvious reasons, but remember that it only becomes relevant if the business fails – if it's successful then there isn't really an issue.

You should be aware that you can borrow up to £25,000 by way of a standard personal loan without having to provide any security to the bank. You could therefore circumvent the security issue by borrowing the money personally and then putting it into the company, rather than borrowing it directly in the company's name.

The other thing to be aware of is that the banks are notoriously reticent in giving back security once you have repaid your loan or overdraft and no longer owe them anything. If you don't owe them anything, there is absolutely no need for them to have any security from you. No doubt they will say "let's leave in place just in case you borrow something in the future", or it's difficult because the documents are stored away in their vaults, but why should they have a call on your home when they don't need one. If you leave the security with them, at any time in the future, whether it's regarding the business or whether it may be a personal debt or even a credit card, they've got you and they can call it in.

Be a pest, hassle them, bug them, chase them, but make sure you get your security either back in your hand or torn up if you no longer owe them any money and don't have a debt to them. It's important, if only to keep the other half happy!

Grants and loans from Enterprise Agencies

You may be surprised to know that there is actually plenty of money around, but you have to know where it is, how to apply for it, and how to present your proposition to gain maximum effect. Once again, you'll need to do your research and try and find these local sources of funding – the Chamber of Commerce is probably a good place to start, but they do exist.

In my local area alone, there is an organisation called Midlands Community Finance, which can lend local businesses up to £25,000 at competitive rates without any security, plus the Derby Enterprise Growth Fund and the Invest to Grow scheme run by Derby University. The DEGF has £20 million from the government and provides grants and loans to local businesses in order to stimulate growth. Invest to Grow has £16 million for businesses throughout the East Midlands on a similar basis. They provide both grants and loans and will lend up to 30% of the proposed 'project' requirement. Invest to Grow has a minimum award of £15,000, so the project needs to be valued at around £50,000.

It's important to get the proposal right before it's submitted, because they will fund the costs of an entire project, including staff costs, exhibitions and marketing, as well as the capital costs.

> A client needed to buy a new machine for just over £3,000 for her business but didn't have the money. Rather than applying for a grant for just the machine she wrapped it up in a funding bid that also included raw materials, manufacture, packaging design, attendance at trade fairs, salaries for personnel to attend the fairs and other things.
>
> In total, it became a £34,000 project and a grant was awarded for just under £11,000; all from needing £3,000 to buy the machine.

Ultimately, these 'funds' are looking to create new jobs and stimulate local economies. They often allow between £10,000 and £13,000 per job created, so if you are asking them for £30,000 of funding, they will want to see you create 2 or 3 jobs over the following couple of years. Many businesses, certainly in the start-up phase, will be doing that anyway and you will count as the first one yourself!

There will be a small amount of due diligence to be done, but it's only fair that a body giving free money to local businesses should make sure it's spent wisely and it's definitely a price worth paying to add to your capital and cash resources.

Start by typing 'growth fund' and 'local enterprise partnership' into Google and see what's available in your area.

Investors and Investment

Otherwise known in the trade as 70% of something can be better than 100% of nothing.

Bringing in outside investment and having someone else own part of the company can be a very emotive subject, and it's only natural that the person whose idea it is wants to keep all the proceeds. By all means, use all your own money, beg, borrow but don't steal it from family and friends, apply for grants, talk to the bank and see if you can raise it all yourself, but you may just find that you still need more in order to make the business work.

I firmly believe that investors are well worth having on board. I've had outside investors in two of my companies and I probably wouldn't have survived without them. The media might call them dragons, but they're not dragons at all, they are keen to see the company succeed (they do have an interest, after all!), they become mentors to you and provide an outside, detached, but more importantly experienced point of view to help with any problems you may need to solve. Outside investors also tend to know lots of people and have a bit of a Midas touch, as they've been there, done it and have a wardrobe full of tee-shirts; a touch that you can seriously benefit from. You'll probably end up with a larger and more successful business with an investor involved.

Obviously, you should try and hold on to as much equity as you can, but you have to be realistic and the more pragmatic you are about it, the better you're likely to get on with the investor, which you'll have to do for the long term. If you haven't enough money to launch the business you haven't got a business and you're not going to succeed without getting access to the money you need from somewhere.

You may think it's unfair that the investor makes a lot of money on the back of your efforts, but you'll make a lot of money too on the back of their money, which they could easily have invested elsewhere.

Ultimately, to work out if it's a good deal for you, do the numbers and see what the business can do with your own resources and how long it will take you to get to a particular point. Compare that to what you think it could do with the investment on board. People often say they could get to that point themselves but it would take five years, but with the investment and investor on board, they could be there much quicker, in two years for example.

That's all very well, you could make it to that point 3 years early, but to fully quantify the investment, you have to look at where you'll be with it in the full five years. The chances are you will be much, much further on than the two year point you were looking at in the first place. After the five years, 70% of something much larger will be worth a lot more than 100% of something much smaller.

To illustrate the point, take a look at some figures as an example.

Year	Growth @10%	Growth @27%
Now	£100,000	£100,000
End Year 1	£110,000	£127,000
End Year 2	£121,000	£161,000
End Year 3	£133,000	£205,000
End Year 4	£146,000	£260,000
End Year 5	£161,000	£330,000

On your own, or with an investor?

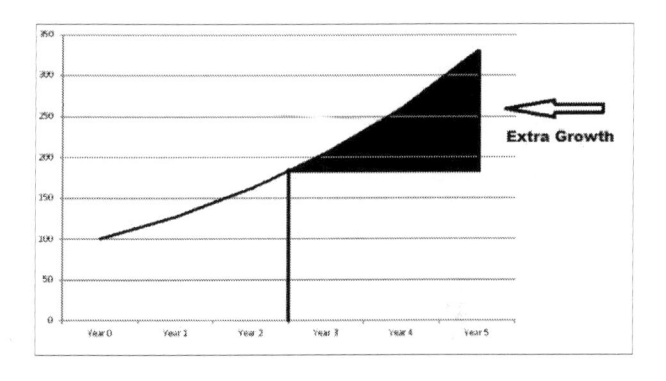

If the business grows by 10% per annum after five years it will be doing 160% of the start point. To get to that point at the end of year 2, the business needs to grow by 27% per annum rather than 10%. If, after the two years, it keeps growing at the same rate of 27% per annum, then by the end of the five year period it will have more than trebled since the beginning and will have more than doubled the original ambition of growing at 10% per annum for five years.

In all likelihood, the growth will be sustainable because, almost naturally, the investor will have been there, done it, have the experience and more importantly the contact base to bring new customers and additional income to the business. Their money is invested in your business, so they have a natural desire to see you do well and succeed, and they will send business your way. Why wouldn't they?

As you can see, getting there in two years allows for significant extra growth and therefore value to the end of the five year period.

In this example, you could own 100% of a business doing £161,000 or you could own 70% of a business twice the size with an investor on board. If that's the case, even though you may have sold 30% of the company for the investment, in monetary terms you'll be 20% better off than if you'd kept everything for yourself.

Given that most businesses are long term projects, extrapolate the figures up to ten years and the figures get larger still. On your own, you'd still only be at £260,000, but over £1,000,000 with the investor and the continued growth. Obviously, there are no guarantees that the growth will continue and carry through, and the numbers that I've used are hypothetical, but there are no guarantees from doing it on your own either.

If we ask the question again with the numbers in there; 70% of over a million pounds, or 100% of a quarter of that? It's your choice.

If one of the reasons you set up the business was for the money, then taking on an investor and making use of their money, expertise and experience could be the best investment you ever make!

The point I'm really trying to make is that you shouldn't close your mind to the idea of outside investment and "giving away" a part of the company. Firstly, you won't be "giving it away", you'll be getting money, experience and expertise for it. Secondly, it will reduce your own financial burden, particularly in the early days and thirdly, it may just make you an awful lot more money than you could make on your own!

Cash, cash, cash

Cash is pretty close to everything that matters when running a business; if you don't have any you can't do anything when you want to, and lack of cash is what often makes companies bankrupt. It's therefore best to try and keep as much of it in the business as possible, especially in the early days. Let me explain.

Given that sales nearly always take longer to come in than expected and the bills have to be paid until the sales finally do roll in, you will almost certainly need more cash than you might think. What you shouldn't do is spend it all in the first couple of months and then have nothing left to cover any delays in sales orders.

> £50,000 is invested in a business that requires a £25,000 machine in order to manufacture its product and a car for the salesperson to visit prospective customers. The company has a couple of staff and monthly salaries of £5,000 per month. They could spend £25,000 on the machine and, say, £20,000 on the car in the first month, but all the money will have

> gone and they'd be bankrupt before they start.
>
> Instead, they lease the car and pay a small monthly amount, take a loan for the machinery and repay it over five years. By keeping nearly all the investment money in the business, it gives them cash to cover the overheads for almost a year and allows the sales team plenty of time to get up to speed.

The same principles apply if you're taking on an investor; the last thing an investor wants to see is their money disappear in no time and then the business need more in order to survive. Once the sales have been sorted out and the business is profitable, you can always repay any loans early but you'll be doing it out of profits, not capital. Yes, you'll have to pay interest on the borrowing, but it can be a small price to pay to keep the capital in the business for much longer, and well worth it.

Flat Rate VAT scheme

It won't make a massive difference to the business, but if your business qualifies to take advantage of the Flat Rate VAT Scheme, then it might be worth looking at. It's intended for small businesses with small turnovers of less than £150,000 per annum and it essentially provides free money from the government. Yes, you heard it, free money from the Government.

Essentially, you're not allowed to claim back VAT on anything you buy, so it's more suited to service industries such as consulting, design, or PR, where they don't buy in a tangible product and resell it. When you sell something, you charge VAT at the normal current rate of 20% on your invoices and collect that VAT in the normal way. The Government then has a list of flat rates of VAT that apply to different types of businesses and that's what you pay them at the end of each quarter, keeping the difference for yourself, as a Government incentive to small businesses. So, if you're an advertising business for example, you pay 11%, if you're in entertainment or journalism you pay 12.5%, labour only building services you pay 14.5%, or a travel agency pays just 10.5%.

> A freelance journalist invoices their clients £10,000 + 20% VAT (£2,000) each quarter. At the end of the quarter, they pay the taxman the equivalent to 12.5% VAT, a total of £1,250, and keep the balance of £750 for themselves. A total of £3,000 over the course of a year for doing nothing but collecting the VAT on behalf of the Government.
>
> Using the same figures, a travel agent would collect £2,000 in VAT from their customers, hand over £1,050 of it to the taxman and keep the other £950. A total of £3,800 over the course of a year.

Whichever way you look at it, if your business qualifies, it's a gift from the Government, no strings attached, and we don't get many of those. It all adds up and if you were successful enough to be invoicing £12,000 per month, for the travel agent it would equate to an extra £15,000 per annum for literally doing nothing.

For full details of the scheme and to see whether you qualify, go to https://www.gov.uk/vat-flat-rate-scheme/overview

Money Recap

→ Structure your capital in a tax efficient way

→ Know your numbers!

→ Look at alternative non-bank funding, grants and loans

→ Don't close your mind to investors

→ Keep as much cash as you can in the business

→ Check out the Flat Rate VAT Scheme and see if you qualify

/3
People

Get the best, not the cheapest

Small businesses tend to start out with a group of like-minded, determined, enthusiastic people who'll do anything to make it succeed. They create a family atmosphere, an all-for-one and one-for-all mentality and will work late, weekends and difficult hours to ensure the business works.

I firmly believe that the people make the business. If one person doesn't care, they let everyone else down and that reflects on the company as a whole. My advice would always be to hire the best people possible, not just the cheapest. Hire people that fill in your weaknesses and will go the extra mile. Whatever you may think as the business owner, you can't do everything and you need people to back you up who you can trust to do their jobs.

After all, it's your business, you've made the sacrifice and investment to get it going; don't you want the best possible chance of not only protecting that investment but multiplying it ten-fold? Average but cheap isn't good enough; go for the best you can possibly afford at the time, all the time.

If you're a product person and not comfortable selling, get the best salesperson possible in order to maximise sales; if you're a salesperson but not a product person, get the best product person possible to make your offering the best it possibly can be and therefore easier to sell. If it's easier to sell, you'll sell more and you'll make more money than the employee will cost you extra. I've seen people whose forte is selling, but they won't let go and spend half the week doing the admin, or the accounts and they limit themselves massively.

> A business turned over £250,000 per annum with a 40% margin but the owner complained he couldn't grow it. He did all the admin and wouldn't let go or employ anyone, so he had just one day a week for selling. It followed that doubling the amount of selling time would double the turnover and also the gross profit.
>
> He listened to advice and outsourced the accounts for £500 per month, spent much more time selling and doubled the turnover and margin. £6,000 per annum invested in getting an expert to do the accounts led directly to an increase in annual gross margin of almost £100,000.

Don't be afraid to give someone a chance

I've always thought that recruiting is one of the hardest parts of running a business. Finding someone with the right attitude is more important than someone with the right skills but the wrong attitude – you can teach the skills, but you can't often change the attitude.

Don't be afraid to give someone a chance either – there are lots of youngsters out there who need a break, so if you can't find the right experience through the normal channels, give a graduate a chance and you may just find that a bit of youthful exuberance and energy go a long way. They'll be keen to learn, keen to impress and thankful that someone has given them the chance.

There are some employers who shy away from training their staff properly because somebody, once upon a time, went on a training course and then left, making the employer resentful they'd paid for the training and then got none of the benefit. Please don't be one of them, grow up, get a life and make sure your employees are properly trained. They will all appreciate the time and effort put into them, they will enhance their knowledge, be more use to you on a day to day basis, and if one does leave, well, you recruited the wrong one in the first place.

Don't treat 99% of your staff badly because the 1% let you down.

If they're good at it, let them do it

The phrase "jack of all trades, master of none" was created for a reason. No-one can be good at everything, so please understand that you're not the best at everything, you just own the company.

You are not the best salesperson, the best product person, the best accountant, the best marketer, the best trainer, the best software developer, the best everything. You might well be the most opinionated person, but that's because it's your business. Recruit people into the business that are better than you are; they are not a threat because you're their employer, and then let them do what they are good at. Why would you hire someone who's a marketing expert and then tell them how to market? You've hired them to do it for you, so let them. Give them the freedom to do their jobs and don't interfere all the time.

They're supposed to be grown, responsible adults who are good at their jobs, so please, please, please let them do it. Don't suffocate them and impose on them as you'll prevent them from doing their jobs to the best of their abilities. It may be difficult, but you have to trust them.

Once you've got them, look after them

In business, people come and people go, but retaining the best staff is much simpler and much cheaper than continually having to find new ones. You will quickly be able to identify the members of staff that are "one of us", who have the right attitude and commitment to the company, and will go the extra mile. These are the ones to keep, so they need to be looked after and put in place for the long term. It doesn't take much to look after people in the right way, and assuming they are paid a competitive wage in the first place, it doesn't usually take lots of money either.

You can look after the right people with gestures of goodwill, compassion, understanding and by cutting them some slack when they need it the most. I've sent people on holiday, with the company paying for it, when they've been working long hours non-stop and are getting close to burn-out. I've sent a group of girls to the races for the day, with a slap-up lunch included, as a thank you for dealing with an office move, including lugging all the furniture around while the guys made excuses, hid in the corners and left them to it.

If someone has been on-site all week, away from home and living in a hotel, tell them to take their other half out for dinner at the weekend and put the bill on their expenses. It doesn't take much for the gesture to be appreciated, it might be as simple as sending them home early on a Friday or letting them go to a private appointment without taking it as holiday.

In return, you tend to get commitment, enthusiasm, a willingness to go the extra mile when necessary and loyalty. They are all traits that are vital to the success of a small business and all things that can't be purchased or taught. It would be easy to say the company shouldn't be paying for holidays or days out, or that it can't afford them, but think about the time and cost of replacing the burnt out employee if they resigned. Adverts, interviews, short lists, second interviews, waiting for the replacement to start and then giving them time to get up to speed. A £5k recruitment fee, three months disruption, all the lost knowledge or a few hundred quid giving them a break? You choose.

It would be cheap at twice the price. It's all about the people, and it's a no-brainer for me. If you look after them, they will look after you, so don't be tight and miserly with them.

The wrong people are destructive

The wrong people don't necessarily destroy the company, that's pretty unlikely, but they will destroy morale and create resentment and animosity between colleagues. For me, there are two types of worker; there are the ones that want a career and strive for better and there are the ones that just want a job, with a salary to pay the bills at home and they don't care less what they do or how they do it. Sadly, it's just a fact of life and there's not really anything you can do about it other than get used to it. Much of it is simply about attitude but it's a modern day problem that people expect a lot for not much effort and seem to have a false sense of entitlement. Not everyone will have the same desire, work ethic or determination that you have to make sure the business is a success.
I believe that once a small business gets to ten or twelve people you start to get some jobs-worth's creeping in and the culture can start to change. Once

you get to that certain size, it seems inevitable that you end up hiring some of them. You have to try and avoid them if you can and maintain the culture of all-for-one for as long as possible.

It's really noticeable in the big corporates where you have the go-getters on one hand and the 9-5'ers on the other. It tends to be why the corporates are rule based, slow to react, and often getting anything done is like wading through treacle, whereas small businesses are nimble, agile, quick to react and get things done much more efficiently.

A tender document for a large deal needed to be submitted by Friday. The document still wasn't finished on Thursday afternoon and in order to get it done staff needed to stay late, not just to get it done but to ensure it was really polished. One of the bid team said "My contract says I only work until 5pm" and promptly went home.

As a result the document didn't get finished properly and the company lost the deal. The offending employee didn't have a guilty conscience because in their mind they'd done nothing wrong – it was their right to go home.

Reflecting on the example above, think about how the others felt, those that did put in the effort, got the proposal together, worked long and hard on it, only to be let down by a colleague who isn't prepared to put in as much effort or lift a finger to help? Think about the salesperson who nurtured the deal possibly for months and now won't get any commission? All their work wasted. Think about the product people who've prepared and done the presentations and now won't get the chance to implement their solution? All their work wasted too. It could mean the difference between a Christmas bonus for everyone, or even a Christmas party, or in the extreme, their salary at the end of the month.

"It's not my job" is a phrase that shouldn't be allowed to exist in a small business as there are times when everyone has to go the extra mile and get it done, for the good of the company, for the good of colleagues, for the greater good as it were.

That said, it is an attitude, so try and avoid hiring it in the first place. Recruitment is one of the hardest parts of business and getting the right people is difficult, but that's why you should try really hard to look after and keep them once you've found the right ones.

Stick with your values

I've already said a number of times that recruitment is one of the hardest things for a business to do well. Each different business needs different people, different qualities and different levels of expertise, so it's not easy to pin down exactly what you have to do to get the right people.

What I would suggest you do is stick with your values and principles as best you can. If you value honesty above all else, make sure you get it; if you value punctuality, make sure you get that, if it's attitude and effort you want, hire that, or if it's pure talent you're looking for, get the most talented even if they look or dress in a crazy fashion. If you stick with your core values and principles, you won't get it right all the time, but you won't go far wrong.

If someone wants to leave, it won't be the money

It's also inevitable that people leave and move on, even the good ones, but it's a mistake to do the obvious thing and pay them more money to stay. People don't tend to leave for money; they leave because they're fed up, dis-enfranchised, bored and unhappy in their job. Unless you change their job, or the circumstances surrounding it, they will still feel the same way three months later and all you'll have done is pay them more money to stay a bit longer. Paying someone to stay is just money down the drain that would have been better spent on recruiting a replacement.

If you give someone a £3,000 pay rise to stay when they threaten to leave, all you'll do is spend £285 per month (£250 salary plus tax and NI) for as long as it takes them to get fed up again, and then they'll leave anyway. It's much better to cut your losses, let them leave and use your money to replace them more effectively.

If someone really enjoys working for the company but just feels they are underpaid, they'll come and talk to you and ask for a pay-rise, meaning you can deal with it before it becomes a leaving problem, assuming you want to keep them of course!

Who's for the longer term?

As I've said earlier, I always had a vision of how I wanted my business to look; how large it was, what it turned over and made, how many people were in each department and such like. I also always had in my mind who would head up those departments and who of the existing staff would be able to step up and manage in a larger, more successful company. I knew who I wanted to take with me. I even had ideas at various stages of who could possibly run the company should I ever choose to take a step back and not work as hard.

Try and have in your mind who you'd like to be with you in five years' time and put time into nurturing them and making sure they can take on the added responsibility when you need them to, without necessarily making promises that one day you might not want to keep. Build your inner circle and allow them to have an input into strategic decisions so they really feel involved in the fabric of the company. Talk to them, get their views and consider them, incentivise them with bonuses based on success whilst always maintaining the right to have the last word and ultimate decision yourself.

Everyone knows how to run it better than you!

If you've ever been to a football match, you'll know that there are always 20,000 better managers and 20,000 better players sat in the crowd watching the game. They all have an opinion, they're always right and they're always calling somebody useless. Of course, there's a reason they're sat in the crowd and not on the touchline or the pitch; they're not good enough to do the job themselves, otherwise they'd be doing it. We all know how to run the country better than the Prime Minister, but we wouldn't want his job, would we?

It's the same in business; everyone knows how to run your business better than you do. There's always an opinion, always a clever clogs, but they never have to take the responsibility for making decisions, live with them or pay for them. There are plenty that like to moan and complain that "everything is rubbish". Try asking them what they'd do instead and the answer will usually be "I don't know" or it will involve spending a pile of money you don't have. The sales team will never have a big enough marketing budget, your development team will never have enough developers and the accountant will never have enough money available because everybody wants the perfect world. They aren't the ones that are responsible for juggling it all, choosing where to allocate the money that is available, when to hire staff or not, and they often don't understand the overall picture.

Again, it's human nature; everyone knows best, but they don't have to take the responsibility for delivering it and living with the consequences. It's very easy to be critical, but if its criticism without a solution, don't take it to heart. I find it very difficult to accept criticism if the answer to "what would you do about it?" is either silence or "I dunno". If people are going to criticise, they should at least make it constructive and come with some answers as well.

As the business owner, expect to be blamed for everything, but not to get any credit for the good things, which will all have been done by the employees. You need to be ambivalent to it, and remember that without you employing them, they wouldn't even have a job!

People Recap

→ Recruiting is one of the hardest things

→ Get the best, not the cheapest

→ Look after them

→ Keeping them is much easier than replacing them

→ Don't pay anyone to stay

→ Don't let the bad ones destroy the rest

→ Who's for the long term and can handle success

→ Don't treat 99% based on how 1% behave

→ They all know better than you!

→ Stick to your values and principles

/4
Sales and Marketing

Nobody knows you're there

It may seem like an obvious thing to say, but nobody knows you're there unless you tell them. I've known start-ups spend years developing products, getting offices, buying cars, employing staff and then they all sit there on launch day waiting for the phone to ring. It's really dis-spiriting when it doesn't because they firmly believe everyone, just everyone, will want to deal with them as soon as they're open for business, but if you haven't told anyone you exist, no-one will call.

Even established businesses need to continually remind their target audience that they exist and make sure everyone knows they're in business and ready to be of service. Sales and Marketing is vitally important and no business will exist for long without doing it effectively. Luckily nowadays, with social media as prevalent as it is, marketing can be done very cheaply, if not free, and the reach you can get is substantial with things like Facebook 'shares' and re-tweets on Twitter.

You have to be sensible but don't let excuses or products get in the way of sorting out the sales and marketing function.

If you're starting up and have a non-compete clause with a previous business, you may not be able to shout about your new business until the handcuffs come off, but you can at least be ready with brochures, a website, literature and promotional materials so that you can hit the ground running on day one.

Get your website done properly

If you've only got the money to get one marketing thing right, then use it to get your website professionally built and done properly. Nowadays, the first thing anybody does when they hear about a new company or a product is head to Google and type its name, and as they always say, you only get one chance to make a first impression.

The world isn't stupid; most people can spot a home grown or amateur website a mile off and it immediately smacks of small, amateur and tin-pot outfit, exactly the opposite of the impression you're trying to create. Unfortunately, there are plenty of tools available that allow sites to be built for free where you just pay for the hosting costs afterwards, so it's easy to think you can just create it yourself. If you do it that way and try to save the money, have a look at your main competitors sites once you've finished and see how you stack up; the chances are you won't look as good, as professional and you might well think you need to get it done properly! You can't do everything, so where your first impression is concerned with a significant amount of the population, get it right. There are, however, common sense ways of mitigating some of the costs of getting a good site up and running.

Pictures and visuals are becoming more and more important in modern day life, we all send pictures and videos from phones to each other and we're all becoming more visual. It's easy to search the internet and buy high quality stock images from places like iStock Photo or Shutterstock, but these tend to get used all over the place and some of them are quite expensive, making it really easy to spend a couple of thousand pounds just buying meaningless standard images that can be found everywhere, with smiley models that everyone knows aren't real.

I always get my images by hiring a professional photographer for a couple of hours. It might cost £200-£300, but that can be the cost of just one stock image and if you've planned out what you want properly, you end up with a library of potentially hundreds of photographs that you own and can use on all your marketing materials for a number of years. Get pictures of your people; if you have call handlers get some pictures of them with headsets on answering the calls, if you have to go and install your product, get some pictures of the installers setting it up in a real environment, if you have a shop, get some pictures of the shop with some customers in it, and so on. Using your own people also personalises things and makes it more real; when a customer walks in the shop they see the person from the website behind the counter, not a photographic model that everyone knows is false. It resonates more and helps to build the relationship between company and customer; they feel like they've already met them and have something to talk about. "I know I'm in the right place, I saw you on the website"

I would recommend it every time; for the price of one or two stock photographs you will end up with an image library of hundreds of real, life-like pictures of your real business that can be used on your website, in brochures, leaflets, postcards and any other marketing materials you may create in the future. You'll have enough pictures that you can refresh things over time as well if you'd like to, showing that your website is continually evolving and changing and isn't just a static site. It is money very well spent.

We can't afford to spend money on marketing?

Many small businesses think they shouldn't spend money unless they absolutely have to, but not spending money on marketing really is a false economy. Failing that, given that everyone is either an expert or a web developer, they decide to do it themselves to save money.

I did some consultancy work for an IT company and when I got there they didn't even have a website – "coming soon – our website is being re-developed" it said on the home page. It wasn't, they just had a really poor sales and marketing function and thought they could get away without spending the money. Cash flow was the next excuse; they couldn't afford it.

Let's get one thing straight – the aim of marketing is to create customers. Period. It builds profile, but ultimately it's there to create customers. Without customers, you don't exist.

They didn't have the cash flow to pay for a new website because they didn't have enough customers. They didn't have enough customers because nobody knew they existed, given the first thing everyone does nowadays is go to Google and looks for a decent website. An IT company without a website doesn't sound like it's going to be around for very long, does it?

Price it for the market, not for you, and target

When pricing your product, think about what it's worth in the marketplace. I've worked with people who I suspect have priced their products based on what they need to earn for a comfortable life, or what they'd pay for it themselves, rather than what the product is actually worth to the customer.

It's human nature, we all have a view on what we'd be prepared to pay for something, but it's unlikely we're the customer for our own business' product and therefore we're probably wrong. Don't price your product for yourself; price it for the market and its worth to the customer.

> A client was in a corporate job and lived a comfortable life on £30,000 a year, but then decided to start his own business. He thought he could sell his product 100 times per annum, so he set the price at £300, allowing him to maintain his comfortable lifestyle.
>
> His product was mainly bought by senior executives of large companies. They used it to help them complete 80% of a major project, which, if done manually, would cost them in the region of £10,000. As such, it wouldn't have been considered unreasonable to charge £8,000 for the product.
>
> From a marketing perspective, in order to give the customer a really tangible saving, he upgraded his product to a £3,000 price tag, which still represented great value for money. The impact of pricing for the market, rather than for himself, was huge and transformed his business.
>
> There are two ways of looking at the results; selling the same product 100 items per annum results in revenue of £300,000 rather than £30,000, or he only needs to make one sale per month rather than 10 to maintain his lifestyle.

It also means that with fewer sales to make, you can target your audience much more precisely and make sure you get the right sales, not just any sale. It will also give you back much more time, because you have fewer products to deliver. Many businesses will grab any sale because they think it means money, but that isn't always the case if it costs more to deliver.

> A guy in a service industry sold his time at an hourly rate. He was busy but felt he wasn't making enough money. His prices were cheaper than his competitors, so the obvious answer was to increase his prices in line with them.
>
> He worried that if he increased prices by 30% he'd lose customers. Yet, given there were justifiable reasons for increasing the prices, it was highly unlikely that he would lose 30% of his customers. In fact, he lost no customers and immediately had the best two sales months in the history of the business. Even if he had lost 30% of his customers, he would still have made the same amount of money but in 30% less time, giving him more time and space to develop the business, take more contracts and increase revenue.

Obviously you have to be conscious of the competition and be in the right ball-park with regard to pricing, but think carefully about what the product is actually worth to the customer, what it can do for their business and price it accordingly.

Remember, there is no law that says you can't earn £300,000 per annum. Why shouldn't you earn it?

Sell products that are profitable

It may sound ridiculous, but there are plenty of businesses that spend a lot of time and money selling products that are just not profitable. This is mainly because they haven't done the numbers and don't know whether their products actually do make a profit when they take into account all the associated costs that go with it.

> Which one would you rather sell? A company had two products, one that made £20 margin for every sale and one that made £100. The sales force put an equal amount of effort into selling each product, even though they had to sell five times the number of the £20 product to make the same amount of money as the £100 product.
>
> A new Sales Director re-focussed the sales effort towards the £100 product, dropped the £20 product and increased profitability by 65%.

For me, it's a basic requirement to analyse products down to this level, because if they make a loss and don't make a positive contribution to the business, there is no point selling them.

> A software company also supplied hardware and maintenance services to its customers, but that meant it needed a team of four engineers to do the work. When the hardware market changed and customers started buying PC's on-line directly from manufacturers, the company found itself with income from hardware services of £80,000 a year, but costs of £130,000 to cover the engineers, spare parts and travel costs.

> In other words, supplying the hardware and maintaining it cost the company in excess of £50,000 a year, so why bother?
>
> The customer liked the idea of a one stop shop, but providing that service was a luxury the company simply couldn't afford. It shut down the hardware side of the business, cut out the losses and focussed on what it did best; software.

The above example was actually in my own company, and it didn't take long to think "hang on a minute, we're actually a software company and it's our software that we sell, so we shouldn't be doing this". We shut down our technical team and stopped providing the loss making service, but if I hadn't known the numbers and analysed our income and expenditure by each department, we could have carried on blindly pouring more money down the drain.

Similarly, you should look at the effectiveness of the salespeople. Sales are what keep a company alive, without them there is no income and by extension, no company, so sales have to pay for everyone in the business, not just themselves.

If you sell £100,000 worth of a product at 25% margin, you make £25,000 gross profit. However, if you have a salesperson to sell it who is paid £20,000, by the time you've paid the employers NI contributions, plus their expenses for going out and selling it, you're making a loss. There will be other people in the business who spend time helping to make that product sell, maybe a helpdesk, an engineer for when things go wrong, so the costs would be higher still.

If a salesperson doesn't even cover their own costs, never mind make a contribution to everybody else's costs, they are not good enough to be in your business and need to be replaced. Either that, or you haven't analysed your product and market well enough and the sales price or margin is wrong and that needs to change. In any event, small businesses cannot afford to carry passengers, whether they be people or products; every person has to make their contribution and every product has to make its contribution too.

Don't get too hung up on the product

If your company is very product focussed, or very technical, don't get so hung up on the product that you forget to actually go out and sell it. I've been guilty of this in the past, being a software developer by trade, without an effective sales person in place on our opening day, but with other staff who were product focussed too. We thought that our past reputations would serve us well and that people would immediately want to deal with us, so we could do without a dedicated sales function to begin with - wrong.

By all means, ensure the product is as good as it possibly can be for the market, but don't forget sales or marketing in the meantime. It's very easy to get into an ever decreasing circle where someone says they'll buy your product if it does X, so you head off to incorporate X. You decide you'll wait until it's finished before you show it to anybody else, and when you do, they ask for Y. You incorporate Y, then go back and show the first prospect, who then think of Z. Before you know it, you're continually working on improving the product and you forget about going out, actually selling it and asking for orders. In fact, showing it to someone new almost becomes a feedback session rather than the sales activity it should be, where you actually ask for an order and get a deposit.

It doesn't look good if you go to a presentation, show off your great product, only for your prospect to ask for a brochure or a fact sheet to show to their superior who's going to have to authorise the expenditure, and everyone looks at each other because no-one has remembered to write it! Be prepared, put the time and effort into sales and marketing and balance it with work on the product.

Being very product focussed is laudable, but it's a dangerous game that creeps up on you, and the only certainty is that you'll eventually run out of money if you don't make sales and generate income. Having the best product is no use to anyone if you run out of money and go bust.

Promotions and generating volume

I might have just suggested getting rid of products and people that don't contribute a profit to the business, but there are some circumstances, particularly in manufacturing industries, where running promotions and selling things at nearly cost price can work in your favour, so it's something you should consider, especially if you're dealing with large volumes that might sell through supermarkets, for example.

> A distribution company sold a product that costs them £1 to buy. The normal selling price was £1.50, so they were making 50p per unit. However if they ordered in batches of 5,000, the unit purchase price would come down to 50p.

> By running a promotion and selling it cheaper at
> £1.20, they managed to get the volume up to 5,000
> and subsequent orders were bought at 50p per unit.
>
> Further promotions kept sales levels high so they were
> able to make 70p per item in a promotion, and £1 for
> anything sold at the normal price. The initial
> promotion might have cut margins to 20p for a short
> time, but the result was increased margins on all sales
> and therefore increased profits for the long term.

They reduced their sales price, but used that to increase the volumes sold, allowing the manufacturing costs to be reduced in order to create more profit. You don't always need to lift the sales price to create profit, you can reduce the cost price instead.

Try and build recurring revenue

Building recurring revenue can be difficult depending on your business, but can be done in all sorts of different ways and can include simply building customer loyalty.

The hardest way of keeping your business afloat is to have to find new customers on an ongoing basis in order to remain profitable. If your product is a one-off purchase with no strings attached, then it's tricky, but try and think of ways you can tie your customers in to some form of subscription service.

Many companies now look to subscription services to completely underpin the business and give them a strong underlying foundation from which to work. Newspaper websites are more and more looking to subscription services, dating websites use them if you want the premium service, LinkedIn (dating for business!) uses it for its premium version, we often subscribe to software nowadays rather than buying the package and even cloud based disk storage is based on subscriptions.

> Business One sells hard disk drives for customers to store their files at a one-off cost of £50. Business Two sells cloud storage for £3 per month and stores their customers' files on servers somewhere on the internet.
>
> Business One has to find new customers to purchase drives all the time, because once someone buys one they don't need another. It doesn't actually know if it will sell anything next month or next year, because it can't guarantee that anybody new will buy a disk drive. As a result, it's always got to keep its foot on the sales and marketing pedal in order to survive.
>
> Business Two, the cloud storage business, knows it will get £3 every month from every subscriber until a customer gives notice to cancel their subscription. With 10,000 subscribers, it is guaranteed to collect (without the need for a large credit control team) £30,000 every month directly into its bank account by standing order, direct debit or card payment. Whilst there are a few cancellations, generally speaking people do not cancel. Just think about gym memberships for a minute; the best customers for the gym are the people who pay each month but never go, and there are always lots of those.
>
> The costs of running the business are £30,000 per month, so it knows it will break even and be able to survive without having to sell any product or find any new customers. The business runs with much less risk and much more comfort because it knows that before it opens the doors every morning the bills are going to

> be paid by the subscribers. As a result, it has a stronger license to be innovative, creative and go after new things more aggressively.
>
> Over time, Business Two also makes significantly more money than Business One. After eighteen months all the subscribers have paid their £50, the equivalent to the disk drive, but continue to pay on a monthly basis. Over five years, Business Two makes £180 from each subscriber, more than treble the income of Business One, who only ever made the initial £50.

If you can't find ways to formally lock people in to longer term contracts, try and build customer loyalty and get it that way. Even my hairdresser knows I'll go and have my hair cut with him at least eight times a year, and whilst he can't guarantee I'll go back to him, he looks to build loyalty from his customers (and we're all creatures of habit anyway). If he can create a couple of hundred loyal customers who all go six to eight times a year, then he has the making of a secure business without having to go out and find new clients all the time.

Recurring revenue is great for businesses; it provides certainty about future sales income and it helps add value to it for when you eventually come to sell. The acquirer also has certainty and can rely on the ongoing income in the future, doesn't have to concentrate on new sales so much and will therefore pay more for the business than they otherwise might.

Sales and Marketing Recap

- Nobody knows you're there unless you tell them
- Home grown websites usually looks amateur, so do it properly
- Marketing is meant to create new customers
- Price your product for the market, not for you
- Make sure each product is profitable
- Don't forget to sell!
- You can increase margins by looking at the cost prices
- Try and build recurring revenue if you can
- Don't forget Sales have to pay for everything

/5
Running it

Recognise you can't do everything

In my view the biggest single mistake small business owners make is they think they can do everything, particularly if it stops them spending money.

They think they'll do the marketing so they don't have to pay anyone else to do it; they'll do the books so they don't have to pay a book-keeper to do it and so on. Whilst I understand and would be the first to advocate that you shouldn't throw your money around, you have to put it into context.

Let's say you take a "wage" of £50,000 out of the business by way of salary and / or dividends; if you do the book-keeping yourself you're effectively a £50,000 book-keeper and paying way over the odds for the job of book-keeping. If you do the marketing too, then the same principle applies. You end up doing it all yourself, pay way over the odds for each task and burn yourself out in the process. You therefore minimise the time spent doing what you're actually good at and you won't be focussed. Out-source the book-keeping, give someone else the responsibility and pay the right price for it. The same goes for all those other jobs that you're not very good at but you still try and do yourself.

In simple terms, do what you're good at, focus on it, and get other people to do what you're not good at. It's actually cheaper. Spend your money wisely, yes, but free yourself up to do the important things, not the mundane grunt work. The chances are you're the most expensive resource the company possesses, so do the things that are the most valuable and worth the most to the company, not the things that other people can do much more cheaply.

If you're the salesman, go out and sell, generate income, and if you're good at it, you'll make far more money that way than by spending your time doing the company admin.

I know the old argument goes that you can't afford to pay all those extra people, but they don't have to be full time, they don't have to be permanent employees, and they don't even have to be on the payroll. Don't spend 3 days per week doing the accounts in a botched way yourself when you could outsource it in half a day a week and get 60% of your time back to do more valuable things. I'd argue you can't afford not to employ them.

You can't do everything, so do what you're good at, and do it well.

Make yourself dispensable

Most people in a job spend half their life trying to make themselves indispensable, thinking it keeps their job safe. Business owners who try to do everything and won't let go must have the same theory wired into their brains, but it's not good if you're the owner.

When are you going to take a holiday? When are you going to relax? When are you going to start to enjoy the rewards for all the hard work, the investment, the risk and responsibility of getting the business off the ground in the first place?

It's easy to forget that you employ your staff to do the jobs they're employed to do, not for you to do them on their behalf. If you get the business structured correctly, and the right people in the right places, you should only need to steer the ship and the business should be able to run on a day to day basis without you.

Nowadays, you're never out of contact for long; broadband, smartphones, email and the internet are everywhere, so it's much easier to stay in touch with the office and much easier to deal with things when it suits. Believe it or not, they even have all these things abroad!

Having got my business established and stable, I then made sure it could run without me; I recruited the right people to the right positions so I knew that finance was covered, training was covered, operations were covered and then all I had to do was steer the ship, rather than run around on the treadmill in the engine room all the time.

For the last twelve months before I sold it, I took an apartment in Spain and actually commuted between there and the UK when the low cost airlines were actually that. I'd buy tickets at around £45-£60 (which is half the price of a decent train fare in the UK), fly off on a Thursday evening, spend Friday, the weekend and Monday in Spain, then get the Monday evening flight back ready to be in the office for 8am on Tuesday morning. I'd deal with business on Tuesday, Wednesday and Thursday morning and then fly back again.

In truth, I was probably more effective during these twelve months than at any other time in the life of the business; I was more focussed in the office, catching up with finance, developers, trainers and operations at set times of the week, making decisions so people could go off and implement them, and then getting away to have time to think, clear my head, but also deal with the things that only I could deal with, in peace and quiet. Yes, business and life merged into one, I'd work at the weekends, or get phone calls on the golf course, but that's just the nature of a small business anyway. It allowed me to think much more clearly, and put things in perspective. Problems seemed much easier to solve when you weren't immersed in them and you could sit and think about them without interruption, with only the birds chirping in your ear and a big blue sky to look at.

Interestingly, it also made the staff more efficient because if they needed my input, they had to ask for it. I wouldn't be there the next day if they didn't ask me straight away, so it meant they had to get things done too and couldn't keep putting things off until 'tomorrow'.

Cash, cash, cash

We've all heard the phrase "cash is king" and it absolutely is in business. You have to make sure you spend it wisely and collect what is due to you as efficiently as possible.

Believe it or not, the biggest single problem with cash flow in a business is the fact that people expect their salaries to be paid every single month, on time. It's usually the biggest cost, very emotive for people, but every four weeks the wages have to be paid. Your staff won't care that you haven't been paid for that big job you did last month because the big company's payment processes are bureaucratic, long winded and they take sixty days to pay their invoices. It's not their problem. Chances are they'll walk out if you don't pay them and then you won't have any staff in the business to function properly.

Businesses can fail because they're successful; they've sold lots of product, bought in lots of stock, had to pay for the stock, haven't been paid for what they've sold, don't have enough money to pay the wages and end up closing down for that very reason.

Don't for one minute think that if you go out and sell lots of product, the cash will look after itself because it won't. You have to be "on it" with regard to payments going out and the cash collection of what you're owed, particularly collecting what you're owed. Be efficient in collecting your debts without being rude.

Monthly numbers

You should know how the business is performing on a monthly basis and the most obvious way of doing that is through the accounts. I always made sure I had the following every month, ideally by the 7-10th of the following month:
- monthly Profit and Loss Account
- Debtors List
- Creditors List
- Cash Flow forecast
- The Order Book

So, by 7th February, I'd have the numbers for January, by 7th March I'd have the numbers for February and so on.

The P&L will show you whether you made a profit last month and how much you're making for the year so far, the Debtors List will tell you how much you're owed, the Creditors List how much you owe, the Cash Flow when it's all going to be collected or paid and whether you've got enough money to cover the wages, and the Order Book gives you visibility of what's to come in the near future. You can add a variation to the P&L by having actual figures up to the current month, and then forecast figures for the rest of the year, showing you how the year should end up if it all goes to plan.

If you have your numbers each month, accurately and on time, you can react to what's going on and put things right before anything gets out of control. You can see if the debtors are due to come in before the creditors have to be paid and that you have enough cash to operate; you can see if the Order Book is low and whether you need to do something to ramp up the sales, or that there is a big VAT bill to pay from the cash flow, which may in turn mean you have to collect some of the money you're owed sooner. You shouldn't ever be surprised by a VAT bill; they happen every three months and the bigger it is, the more successful you've been, so don't knock it. It's not your money; you've just collected it on behalf of HMRC.

The point is that if you have the information you can do something about it, but if you're blind to what's actually going on in the business you can't.

I know a business that doesn't really bother with the accounts, and they only really know how much profit they've made when their accountant presents their year-end figures to them. This means they only have an accurate picture once a year, at a point when it's already too late to do anything about it. They run their business simply based on whether there's enough money in the bank at the end of the month to pay themselves and if there is, that's fine. Not surprisingly, they just drift along without any real knowledge of where they're making profit, what they're making profit on and how much their costs are. They don't react to anything that's happening in the business or fix any problems because they're not monitoring any of it and are largely unaware. In my opinion, they're not running their business at all, it's running and controlling them; they're wandering along blissfully ignorant of what's actually going on.

Be aware of your costs and buy things well

You also need to be aware of your costs and make sure you buy things wisely and well. Whilst the largest costs in most businesses tend to be people and offices, spending money just reduces profit and if you're not buying things as cheaply as possible you can waste an awful lot of money. Believe me, it's amazing how much things add up to if you don't buy them well.

> A lazy internet based distribution business sent its products out in cardboard boxes every day of the week. It took the easy way out and bought the boxes conveniently from the local Staples store, where each box had a retail price of £3.91. A smart distribution business doing exactly the same thing spent two minutes searching Google and found the same size box on a wholesale website for £1.55. It was even smart enough to go through a website called www.topcashback.co.uk and got another 9.45% cash back as well. Both businesses sent out five items per day, not unusual for a distribution or eBay business, but the smart one saved £12.55 per day, or £62.75 per week, or £3,263 per year, just by buying the boxes better.
>
> To ship them, the lazy business simply used the best known courier firm, but the smart one spent another two minutes on the internet and found two reputable

> courier firms that were £8.21 cheaper to ship the same parcel to the same place within 48 hours.
> Extrapolating the figures again for 5 items per day shows the smart business saved a further £41.05 per day, £205 per week and therefore £10,670 per year.
>
> The smart business bought things well and cut its costs, just for boxes and shipping, by £14,000 per annum.

Just by buying well and taking the time to search for better deals rather than convenience, the smart business added almost £14,000 per year to profits just by reducing its shipping costs. It's true that lots of little things add up to big money and if you can find five or six things within the business and buy them better, you can make a significant difference to profitability.

The Top Cashback website is well worth a look (www.topcashback.co.uk) as a good example of where lots of little things can add up to a lot. Basically, it passes back to the consumer the commission it receives from retailers for sending traffic to their websites. All sorts of retailers are on there, but the biggest commissions are for high margin purchases where the costs are small, such as phone contracts, insurance, breakdown cover and hotel rooms. That said, you can get cashback on common business expenses such as train fares, car hire and even flights as well.

> The smart business also had a sales force that travelled around and had lots of hotel stays; averaging a total of ten hotel nights a month. Just by using the Top Cashback website and then choosing Expedia, they usually got 12.5% cash back on all their hotel

> bookings, and if it's £100 for each night, that's £125 per month, or £1500 per year saved for the sake of a couple of clicks.

If you do go and sign up to Top Cashback, do it with this link (www.topcashback.co.uk/ref/RobEngland) and at least I'll get some credit for it!

It all adds up and if nothing else it might just pay for the Christmas party!

Be organised and tidy

If you're running a business, you have all aspects of it on your mind; the sales and marketing, the finances, the products, resources, staffing and everything in between. It's difficult to keep it all in your head, so try and be tidy and organised.

Write things down, make lists, keep notes and make sure you know what's going on. It's a similar principle to knowing your numbers; if you're disorganised and have no idea what's going on in your own business, how much confidence can anyone else have in it?

In reality, everyone needs to be organised and your internal systems and processes need to be efficient too; the last thing you want are invoices not going out because nobody told the accountant, or everybody thought somebody else had done it, but nobody did. Not knowing, not being able to find things or items being missed because people make assumptions will trip up other aspects of the business; sales may not be able to close a deal because they haven't got a contract, accounts won't be able to invoice if they aren't given the order and customer service can't function if they don't know which products the customer has.

Partially, it's also about image and impressions; if you have a shop and it's untidy with things everywhere, the chances are customers won't be able to find what they're looking for and will go elsewhere; if the staff are untidy, poorly presented and look like they don't care, it doesn't leave a good impression and the customers will vote with their feet and go elsewhere.

If you're organised, tidy and presentable the customer has no reason to go elsewhere and you will leave a favourable impression.

Time – Friend or Foe?

Modern day life sees most people running around saying they're really busy, but they never seem to achieve very much. It's almost a badge of honour to be busy; often the first thing a friend will ask when they see you is "are you busy?" There are an awful lot of people running around busy being busy, when in reality they are just rubbish at managing their time and prioritising. A lot of people just aren't organised and tidy.

Most small business owners would say there isn't enough time in the day and there's always something else to do, so if that's the case, make sure you deal with the most important things, the most valuable things, and don't waste your time with the trivial and mundane. Most people will try and ignore dealing with things they're not comfortable with, hoping they'll just go away, which they won't, and will fill their time with other things instead.

Many years ago I was on the road a lot, was really busy, but just couldn't get anything done. One day, whilst sat on the motorway again, I looked at the trip meter in the car and realised how many miles I'd done. Then I looked at the trip computer which told me my average speed. If I'd done X miles at Y average miles per hour, then I knew how many hours I'd spent in the car over the period of time. I soon realised why I was getting nothing done; I was spending two whole working days every week sat in the car doing nothing but driving. I was only actually working a three day week! That day, it changed.

Time is the one thing you can never get back. Once it's gone, it's gone and a business costs money to run every minute of the day. If your business is profitable, then the profits can give you the luxury of time to plan properly, get things done in the right way and launch new initiatives knowing that they don't necessarily have to come off and you'll still be fine. Time is your friend and allows you to be bold and take some risks.

However, if your business has costs of £10,000 per month, you spend roughly £500 every single day just existing. If you only make £300 on Monday, you've got to make £700 on Tuesday, but if you only make £400 on Tuesday, you've got to make £800 on Wednesday to catch back up again and you still need to make another £500 on Thursday and again on Friday just to stand still.

If the business is making a loss, or not meeting its sales figures, then time is your enemy. Everything just gets harder and the stakes get higher, the amount needed to recover the position back to break even gets larger. If sales stuck at £300 per day for just two weeks, you'll be £2,000 behind the target and getting, literally, worse by the day. £1,000 short of your sales figures each week equates to £50,000 per year and suddenly the impact is very clear. Of course, as the owner, that's £50,000 of your money that you don't have.

The above example is just another reason to make sure you're on top of the numbers and you know what's going on in the business. The sooner you deal with any negative issues, the more time you give yourself to put them right, the easier they are to put right. Deal with the sales issues shown above after one week and you've got £1,000 to claw back, but ignore them, hope they'll go away and deal with them eventually and you'll have a much bigger problem to deal with.

Fight your corner against the big boys

All small businesses look to win contracts with big companies as it gives prestige and can lead to large contracts that are particularly lucrative. There is, however, another side to dealing with large corporations, government departments and multinationals. They often look to impose or bully small businesses into doing everything on their terms. They try and insist on using their terms and conditions that have been written especially in their favour, their ideal pricing and the threat of not winning the deal is often enough for the small business to compromise and give in.

Don't allow yourself to be bullied; fight your corner and don't agree to anything that isn't to the benefit of your business, or that you know you can't deliver. You'll often find it's just an attitude they have in order to get their own way, but you should stand up to them and be firm.

A small adjustment in pricing might make a big difference to you, but is probably less than they spend on coffee in a month and doesn't actually matter to them. They'll ask because, firstly, they should be buying well and secondly, we all need to feel like we've got a good deal, don't we?

You could explain that by reducing the price you'd be compromising on quality, or service, and that would prevent you from doing the best job you could, meaning they wouldn't get the quality they were looking for. Most reasonable people, including buyers, do understand that you have to make a profit and they'll respect you more if you explain your side of the story and don't give in to them.

> A Government department insisted a supplier spent around £10,000 changing its telephone system so they could measure that their phone calls to the supplier were answered within 30 seconds. The supplier refused but was told they had to do it because it was in the contract. They only received 7 calls a day from those Government customers, just one an hour. The contract was completely over the top and far too bureaucratic.
>
> The supplier suggested an on-line survey to ask the customers if they were getting the right level of service, didn't spend the money changing the phone system and still won the contract.

Much cheaper, much less disruptive and much more effective, but just as importantly, it saved the company £10,000.

> A major international bank stated from the outset that a contract for software provision had to be done with their terms and conditions, which were never changed. The supplier was told to "Don't even think about asking for amendments". One of the clauses, however, stated that if there was a problem the supplier had to be on-site to fix it within 2 hours, which was simply impossible from their office location, either by car or train.
>
> The supplier fought their corner, told the bank they had always known the office location and the only way to deliver on the contract clause was to employ someone based close to the bank or move the office. Neither option made any financial sense given the size of the contract. Again, the bank relented, their lawyers changed the contract and the supplier committed to be on-site the next working day for a call in the morning, or the day after for a call in the afternoon.

Contracts

All businesses will have to deal with contracts at some stage of their lives, but remember they are there to protect you. It would be nice if we could all just shake hands, agree something, and both parties would keep to their word, but we're way beyond that nowadays. If you're doing business with friends, or people you get on well with, you may feel that contracts aren't necessary and you should just get on with it. It's easy to say "oh yes, we'll do that, I promise, there's no need to put it in a contract".

Remember that a contract is there for when you and the person you're negotiating with aren't around anymore, and other people, who weren't there when it was written, need to understand what was intended in the first place.

> A salesperson did a deal with the Chief Buyer of a customer. Because they'd known each other for years they agreed everything verbally without a written contract. It was a long term deal that operated over 3 years and had price increases at each anniversary. After nine months the salesperson left the company and after eleven months the Chief Buyer left the customer. After twelve months the company's accounts department sent a new invoice for the increased price, but it was refused because the customer didn't know anything about it.
>
> The contract stayed at the original price and the inflationary increase was lost because there wasn't anything in the (non-existent) contract. That, in turn, reduced the company's sales and margins for the next two years.

Putting a contract in place in the first instance isn't threatening to anyone, it's just writing down what everybody understands the deal to be to prevent issues later on when the original deal-makers aren't around. Don't be embarrassed about asking for a contract to be put in place if you feel it's necessary to protect your business. They don't always need to involve lawyers, or be too complicated, and can often be put together in one or two A4 pages. In some respects, it's back to being tidy and organised again. A small amount of time getting things right at the point of sale can save a lot of trouble down the line.

In five years' time, when the deal is up for review, you may be lying on a beach, with someone running your business for you, so do you really want to be disturbed with the trivia of who said what to whom, and when?

Running it Recap

→ Don't do everything yourself

→ Make yourself dispensable

→ Make sure you collect what you're owed

→ Get your monthly numbers

→ Be aware of costs and buy things well

→ Be organised and tidy

→ Don't be bullied by the big boys

→ Contracts are for when you're not there

/6
Ongoing Strategy

No business in the modern age can just carry on doing what it has always done; it will have to adapt, change and react to the market. Innovation continues apace and change happens very quickly nowadays, so nobody has the luxury of being able to rest on their laurels and coast along. Standing still is not an option.

As a result, you need to continually work on your ongoing strategy and keep looking at what the business needs to do in order to stay in the market and ahead of the game.

Take time out to think

When you work in the business all the time, know all the detail, always have an opinion because you own it, interfere in everything because you're always right, it's very easy to get so immersed in it that you can't see the wood for the trees. There is a famous saying that "you're too busy working **IN** the business to work **ON** the business" and it's very true.

If you don't work to make yourself dispensable, there will always be too much to do, something to get involved in and you'll concentrate on mundane day to day issues that aren't actually important in the overall scheme of things, especially if it helps to put off essential things that you just don't like having to do or aren't comfortable with.

It's very easy to get too bogged down in the detail, but as the owner, you need to have and see the bigger picture, know where you want to go and plan the way to getting there.

It's important to take time out of the day to day grind and just …… think. There are very few things that won't really wait a couple of days, so you can have time to sit back, reflect and think about where the business is going. Get away from home and the office, go somewhere different and sit down and think about the different parts of the business and how they're doing. Ask yourself the questions as if you were an outside consultant asking you, as the owner, how things were at the moment.

Are sales OK? What can be done to improve them? Does it need money or marketing? Where can it come from? Are we collecting our debtors quickly enough? Why are we getting complaints? How can we make things better? Have we got the right people? What are we missing?

Think about the ideal solutions and work back to a solution you can deal with and implement; it might not be the perfect one, but it will take you towards it and will start to improve things. Many of your thoughts may revolve around the people and you may think things such as "I need operations to do it this way, but my Operations person wouldn't be able to do that", which leads you to either a training issue, a personality issue or you might just have the wrong person in the wrong job, in which case, you'll need to put another plan in place to deal with that much bigger issue.

I was lucky when I was commuting to and from Spain because I got away every weekend and it became a continuous process for me, looking at the different aspects of the business, thinking about how we could make them better and then getting on and improving things. I certainly didn't coin the phrase "blue sky thinking", but I could certainly relate to it sat on my balcony, looking out over the Mediterranean with a big warm, sunny sky above me.

You may not be able to do the same, but even if you get away just once a quarter, it's well worth cleaning out your mind and refreshing your thoughts and plans.

A new strategy every year

Following on the same theme, it's a good idea to sit down at the end of one financial year and create the strategy and targets for the next financial year. I had investors in my business, so I used to create a strategy document towards the end of each year that reflected on the year just ending and looked ahead at what we wanted to do with the business in the next twelve months.

It meant we could look back over the past twelve months, see how far we'd come, whether we'd achieved our aims and put into context the progress we'd made. You could also give yourself some credit sometimes, because if you only ever look forward and chase a target that continually moves further away, taking stock and seeing how much you've actually progressed is a good thing.

It's useful to write it all down for a number of reasons; firstly it gives you a reference document to work from yourself, it keeps the investors on-side and allows them to see where things are, plus it helps to educate the staff and let them see the direction of the business as well. You may not show it all to the staff, you might leave out the detailed financials, for example, but having a clear strategy for the business and conveying it to the employees helps pull everyone in the right direction. They will, of course, want their input as well and they might well disagree with some of it!

If you have any kind of relationship with the bank, such as borrowing or a secured overdraft, the chances are they'll want to review everything periodically with you too. Having the strategy document shows them that you have done your homework, know your numbers, know where you're going and are running the business diligently. Having done it in advance also means you don't have to make up a raft of figures and create the plan quickly when the bank call and say "let's get together on Friday".

Make recruitment decisions early

Having a forward view of where the business is going for at least a year in advance also helps you to make decisions early. If you haven't thought it through in advance, then you'll end up making knee jerk reactions that are more risky than they need be.

As far as staffing is concerned, you should ideally be going out on the recruitment trail well before everyone says "we're too busy, we need more people now". If this happens, it's already too late. By the time you've put an advert together, got a job description sorted out, published the advert either on-line or in a newspaper or magazine, you can bet your life that two weeks to a month have gone by. From there, candidates have to put their CV's together, submit them, and you'll have to allow at least two to three weeks for CV's to come in before you can even think about arranging interviews. First interview, short list, second interviews and then appointing the right person will mean you're the best part of three months down the line from when you made the decision to hire them. Should they accept, they might have to work a month's notice before they finally join you, and then once you've trained them so they're actually useful to you, or given them time to get up to speed, you'll be six months down the line from when you started the process. The danger is that you realise you need them too late and stagnate in the period before they come in, giving them a harder start once they do actually arrive.

It's important to realise that new employees don't necessarily become useful the moment they join the company; salespeople need time to learn the products, work up some prospects and then close some deals. If you're a product based company, it may take you three months to train them before they become properly effective. If you are recruiting because the existing workforce are too busy, remember that a new employee could well be a hindrance in the early days too, asking simple questions, bugging people and needing help simply because they don't know how the business works yet.

It won't be like this for all jobs and all types of employees, but it shows how important the plan can be, and how important it is to decide early to get on with the process. If you're hiring them speculatively, on the understanding, for example, that once a particular deal comes in you can afford the extra person, then you can at least get as far as knowing who you'd like to appoint before having to jump in with both feet. If the deal doesn't come off, you can always choose not to appoint, but you'll be a long way ahead of the game if you do decide to go ahead.

Let Go!

It's easy to summarise my tips for running the business on a day to day basis:
- Recognise you can't do everything
- Spend your time on the important and valuable things, not the trivial and mundane
- Do what you're good at and do it well
- Make yourself dispensable
- Take time to think
- Drive the strategy, don't do all the work
- Make decisions early

If you get the business structured properly and allow the right people to do the right things, you should be able to find some time to enjoy the fruits of your labours, rather than be consumed by them. If you can get to that point, then it really will be about the bigger picture, driving the strategy and not getting worked up by some of the petty trivia.

Oh, one last thing

Just when you thought you'd got it all under control and everything was running smoothly, something will always crop up and kick you in the teeth. It just seems to be the way, but something will always come up to challenge you, disrupt you, or make you take a step back before you can take more steps forward.

It could be anything; someone deciding to leave, a good customer going to another supplier, one of your suppliers not being able to deliver on time for a big contract, you just never know. But expect to be hit by some unexpected things along the way. It will happen.

Ongoing Strategy Recap

➤ Create the time to think

➤ Review strategy every year

➤ Make decisions early

➤ Be prepared for the unexpected

➤ Let Go!

/7
Selling it

Selling all or part of your business is a whole new minefield. Money is always a subject that makes people go funny in the head, and nowhere is it more focussed than when you're selling your life's work. People can have really crazy ideas of the value of their businesses and a lot of them are totally irrational and ridiculous.

The first draft of the book ended up with this "Selling it" section being 25% of the total size, somewhat out of sync with a guide that is supposed to help you set up and run your business, not sell it. As a result, I decided to provide a summary here and then produce another pocket guide to cover the "selling" subject. So if you'd like more detail on the minefield of selling your business, pick up my *"Pocket Guide to Selling your Small Business"*.

Be Realistic

Businesses are not always valued on what they're actually worth on paper, or what you might want to sell it for, they can also be valued on what they're worth strategically to the buyer. Whatever price you are looking for, be realistic or you'll simply be laughed out of every meeting you attend. Furthermore, as soon as you come up with a ridiculous valuation you will immediately lose your credibility and the deal will either disappear or the price will inevitably go down.

> A guy wanted to sell his business for £100,000. A prospective buyer asked him why he thought it was worth that and he replied that it was the amount he needed to pay off a loan and his mortgage, leaving him debt free.

> It was a nice and convenient figure, but the business was worth nothing like that. The seller immediately lacked all credibility and not surprisingly he failed to sell his business.

We've all seen budding entrepreneurs on Dragons Den walk in with a great idea, a brand new business without any sales, profits or track record, saying they want £100,000 for 10%. Sadly, it's the delusion of their valuation that often loses them the deal. How can any business that hasn't even started trading, hasn't made a penny in profit and doesn't have any money be worth £1m? Of course, they'll start talking about potential and what it will be worth in five years' time, but that's five years' time, not NOW, and it might not even get there without the investors' money.

If you're selling, put yourself in the buyers' shoes for a second – would you walk into a car showroom and buy a £20,000 car for £50,000, just because the salesman thinks it would be great to get more? No, you wouldn't, so why would anyone pay it for your business? It's exactly why the replacement window industry has such a poor reputation and no credibility; they tell you it's £30,000 for your new windows and then one phone call to their "manager" later and it's "if you sign today Sir, you can have them for £10,000". Who are they trying to kid? We weren't born yesterday!

Don't be too greedy

It's very easy for entrepreneurs to get hung up on the big numbers and hang out for an unrealistic exit point. If you have a ten person company that makes £100,000 per annum in declared profits and has few assets, please don't get prissy, stick your head in the air and say "I'm not selling for less than £5 million!" You can if you like, but that's all you will be doing because you won't be getting the money. If the cost base is going to stay the same and the business is going to carry on trading, it would take the acquirer 50 years just to get their money back, so it isn't going to happen.

A cheque focusses the mind

Believe me, a cheque focusses the mind. You can hold out for the big numbers all you like, but when somebody puts a cheque in front of you and tells you it can go into your bank account today and you can start spending it tomorrow, it's very tempting. Hold out, argue, try and negotiate too hard and the deal may fall apart, meaning the cheque will never go in the bank. Be sensible and put your ego away, at least whilst you're negotiating. You have to play this one in the real world with a cool head, not in fantasy land like a drama queen.

Should I stay or should I go?

This isn't a tough one for me given my past experiences, but if you're selling to a much larger company, just go! Leave. If you're a small business kind of person moving from running your own show to the rules, pettiness and politics of the corporate world won't work. It wasn't for me, and it probably won't be for you either. I've done it twice now and both times I absolutely hated it and had to leave. In my defence, I didn't have much choice as both acquirers tied me in to three year contracts as a key employee and I had to serve my time, but that's exactly how I felt, serving my time like I was in jail.

The reality is that you will, in all likelihood, see the baby that you created, built and nurtured, changed beyond recognition and possibly destroyed before your eyes and believe me, it hurts. It's hard to come to terms with the fact that once you've signed the paperwork, sold the business and taken the money, you are no longer in control and the new owners will run it to suit themselves without any regard for your feelings.

The Actual Sale Process

If you're lucky enough to get an offer for your business that you accept, then get ready for a roller-coaster ride from acceptance to the day the deal is actually done.

The acquirer will undertake a due diligence process to make sure they are getting what they think they're getting and at a fair price. They will take your accounts apart, they will want to see every signed contract that you've got, they'll ask all sorts of questions, they'll want to see customer lists, debtors, creditors and you'll spend a lot of time with your lawyers.

You have to continue running the business as if the deal isn't happening (because it might not), but mentally you start allocating the money and thinking about what life will be like afterwards. You get torn between the present and the future, but you have to live in the present. Much of what you need to do for the sale ends up being done in the evenings with no-one around, and you start going to meetings without telling people where you're going, inventing things to keep the staff away from the truth.

The pressure of running the business full time and trying to sell it at the same time is intense; I have to admit that when we sold the last business I took my eye off the ball in the day to day running and sales weren't as good as they should have been. If the deal had fallen through we'd have had a serious cash flow issue to deal with. I couldn't deal with both things at the same time; couldn't devote the time needed to the sales team and they suffered whilst I focussed on the most important thing to me at the time; the deal to sell the company. If only I'd taken my own advice and made myself dispensable!

Get your house in order

The due diligence process will go through your company with a fine tooth comb, so if you are looking to sell in the near future it really does pay to get your house in order from an accounting and administrative point of view. I'm sure many small business owners don't know where their statutory books are stored, or even what they are, whether they're up to date, or whether all the shareholders have actually got share certificates for their stakes or not.

Get your contracts in order; not just Word document versions that aren't signed, but proper paper copies with a real signature on them, not just from one side, but from both sides. Make sure you own all your intellectual property and make sure the staff contracts sign over all IP rights to the business. Prepare yourself for lawyers, meetings, lots of details and more expense than you might think.

It takes a lot of work to sell a business and our costs, by the time we'd finished with lawyers, accountants, corporate finance people, tax advice and such like were £60,000.

You also need to be completely above board with everything about the business, be honest and don't try and hide any skeletons in the cupboard. You will be asked to sign warranties that confirm you have told the acquirer the truth, the whole truth, and nothing but the truth. If they find anything after the event that hasn't been disclosed or carries a financial burden, they will have the ability to come back at you, potentially up to the value of the entire deal and claim back their money.

The warranties usually last for up to three years, but are contract dependent, and warranties for tax issues, where the company may be liable for tax, can last for up to seven years because that's how long the Revenue have to claim them back. It really isn't worth trying to hide things, because if they come back to you and you've spent the money, you're the one with the problem.

Selling it Recap

- Be realistic and don't be greedy
- Think carefully about staying afterwards
- Get your administrative house in order
- Pick up a copy of my "Pocket Guide to Selling your Small Business"

/8
Remember…

The problem with the mega-rich TV entrepreneurs is that we only ever see the up-side, but they have all put in the effort, made the sacrifices, gone without and taken risks to get where they are. They all still have crazy schedules and hardly ever get the chance to breathe, but now they have the financial rewards to go with it. The fact is they choose to do it now, because they are certainly wealthy enough to take it easy should they wish to do so.

All our ambitions are different, we all have different motivations and energy levels and you can still be a successful entrepreneur without the mega-bucks, so long as you've satisfied yourself and achieved the things you originally set out to do.

It's a long hard road, it doesn't happen overnight but it is incredibly rewarding. They say that nothing worth doing in this world is ever easy, and running your own business isn't.

Remember though, that it's your money and you can spend it however you like. I remember wanting to do something a bit brash once, but said to my business partner that I wasn't sure we should be using company money for it. He duly reminded me that it was our company, we owned it, therefore it was our money and if that's what we wanted to spend it on, we could. So we did! His point, though, is right. It's yours to do with whatever to choose.

Whatever your business, enjoy the journey. Once you get to your destination, wherever it may be, enjoy the rewards.

I hope there's been something in here that will help you on your way. Good luck!

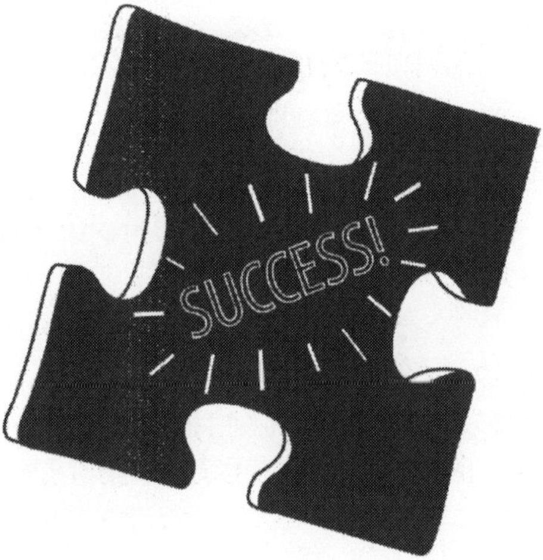
SUCCESS!

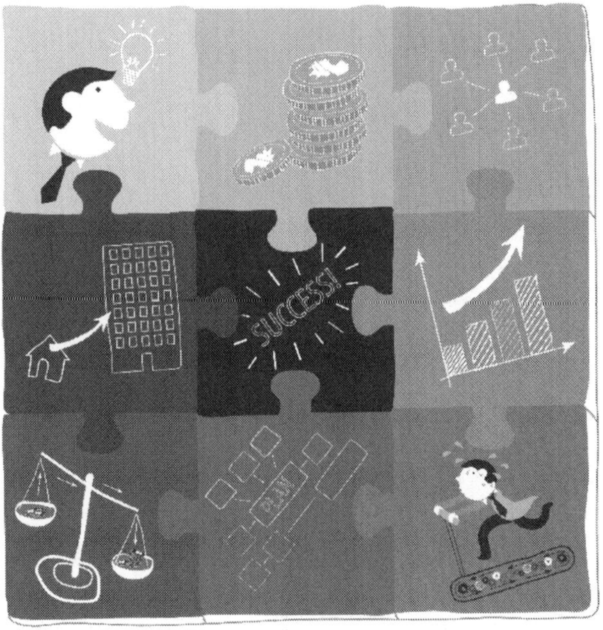
SUCCESS!
PLAN

Acknowledgements

Firstly, I'd like to thank Brian Bickerstaffe, John Holmes and Dr Mike Waldron for believing in me, trusting me with their money over a lot of years and helping me along the way. Without their help and guidance I wouldn't be where I am today and wouldn't be qualified to write this book. As I've already said, it really helps to have a mentor and a shoulder to lean on.

I'd also like to thank Will Hives of Alt-Design (www.alt-design.net) for the illustrations and cover design and Jackie Brewster, writer and editor, for her thoughts, comments, advice and help in getting it finished and ready for publication.

You could always hire me

Since writing the Pocket Guide to Small Business Success I have been contacted by a number of people looking for help with their businesses.

I offer a range of tailor-made, affordable services and ongoing consultancy packages to help you build and manage your business. I fully understand that new and growing businesses may well be strapped for cash, but my rates are reasonable and negotiable dependent on your needs and budgets. In any event, I would expect to add enough by way of advice, changes and introductions to more than pay for my services.

If you would like more information or to get me on board, then please visit my website at www.robengland.co.uk or email me directly at r88england@gmail.com.

I look forward to hearing from you.

About the Author

Rob England is a business consultant and mentor based in Derby, in the UK.

He transferred his youthful sporting competitive spirit into business once injuries piled on the pounds and began his first business at the age of 23. He has been involved in three start-ups over the past 25 years and has sold two of them successfully.

He is a software developer by trade and has created three separate applications from scratch for the healthcare sector, computerising the clinical records of GP surgeries, hospices, private practice and community trusts not only in the UK but also overseas. In time, he employed developers to write the software and ran the company instead.

He hates the politics, pettiness and inability to get anything done in large corporate companies and is very much a small company person, preferring to make decisions and get things done to endless meetings and deciding nothing.

He is married to Claire, has a son and two stepdaughters and loves relaxing at his Marbella apartment overlooking the Mediterranean.

Printed in Great Britain
by Amazon.co.uk, Ltd.,
Marston Gate.